THIS SHARPENING

ALSO BY ELLEN DORÉ WATSON

Ladder Music
(New York/New England Award)
Alice James Books, 2001

We Live in Bodies
Alice James Books, 1997

Broken Railings
(Green Lake Chapbook Prize)
Owl Creek Press, 1996

The Alphabet in the Park: Selected Poems of Adélia Prado
(translations)
Wesleyan University Press, 1990

This Sharpening
Copyright © 2006 Ellen Doré Watson

ISBN 10: 1-932195-43-2   ISBN 13: 978-1-932195-43-9
Printed in Canada

First paperback edition
June 2006
Library of Congress Control Number: 2005911084

Tupelo Press
Post Office Box 539, Dorset, Vermont 05251
(802) 366-8185
www.tupelopress.org

Cover and book design by Josef Beery
Cover photo, *Ice Storm* by Jorge Delucca Jr. © 2005

THIS SHARPENING

POEMS

ELLEN DORÉ WATSON

T P

TUPELO PRESS

ACKNOWLEDGMENTS

I am grateful to the editors who published these poems sometimes
under other titles and in earlier versions:

JOURNALS

American Poetry Review: "Almost," "Free Will," and "Not a Sweater"
Barrow Street: "Warp of Door, Proximity of Darkening"
Boulevard: "Per Se" and "Sunday Morning"
Cimmaron Review: "Petals in the Dirt" (as "Those Petals")
Cortland Review (online): "No Longer Mine"
Field: "Rib(cage)" (as "Funny Rib(cage")
New Letters: "Our Species Alone" (as "Human Chores")
Poet Lore: "Yes from No" (as "Movie Version")
Poetry Northwest: "Earth is Where"
Smartish Pace: "Between Us"
Water~Stone: "Slow Rapids" (as "I am Somewhere")

ANTHOLOGIES

"First Date in Twenty-five Years"– *Never Before: Poems about First
   Experiences* (Four Way Books, 2005)
"Ghazal"– *Ravishing Dis(Unities): Real Ghazals in English*
   (Wesleyan University Press, 2000)

Deep thanks to dear friends and early readers of these poems –
Amy Dryansky, Marsha Janson, Mary Koncel, Margaret Szumowski
– and of this book – Annie Boutelle, April Ossmann,
Catherine Barnett, and Barbara Ras.

And to Della for all she is.

for my father

CONTENTS

THREE

FOUR

FIVE

ONE

Dance with the Devil

When someone is truly but not absolutely every-
thing to you, does that make him the boundary,

this beautiful row of stones? Is it too late or too
good to bend the rules? I don't want to be a fence!

I could let my man blur the lines, says one corner
of my mouth, and the other: nobody says that unless

they're doing the blurring. Chances are the radiance
I'm toying with won't warm my hands, it's light

without content, magic in search of audience.
But I've got hives from dreaming of new tongues,

simply thinking the word gamble. How could the odds
favor this new stew when that couple fell from the sky,

leaving their boy a statistic in the cold? Whoa—
danger, whoa—history. Whoa—that sweet gumdrop

at the center of any family storm. When in doubt,
bring home the groceries. Then the devil saunters in:

Define risk, he purrs. *Pressed to the wall,*
you'd give up every stray thought for them,

am I right? (Or is it the God in me talking?)
The wall is blow-me-away not there until it is.

Free Will

It's there for the taking, like wild blueberries —
a trifle more sour than we remember. It's what we
grown-ups teach our children, taking a machete
to excuses. It's about choice — the sky's the limit,
blah blah, no price tag but beware the price. Once

upon a time a boy wandered off to a stony place
and found himself surrounded by snakes who
happened to be discussing free will. Do you need
to ask what happened? Does it matter that he died
a wiser boy? Does it interest you that the head snake

was the dissenter, urging restraint — would it change
anything to know that the snake who did the choking or
unleashed his poison (we weren't there, the latitude's
not specified) had been abandoned in the egg, taunted
in his youth, had prior knowledge of the boy's stick-

wielding ways and pointed scorn towards reptiles?
Would you breathe easier to know the other snakes
took to shunning or ate his children, turned him over
bloody to the authorities, or if he felt a little sorry?
All a yes proves is you're not that boy's mother.

Sweet But

When birds caw they caw at me scolding because they know
I'm bad or cause they need help I'm just never sure which or
where is the broken-winged lump of coal feathers the perfect
barely blue egg that rolled away like the stone in the story
and who will believe the miracle if I find the egg tiptoe it back
to the nest and will the smell of me condemn it the way my hands
do the dishes chip crack I am also dangerous to my teeth & shins
this is the movie in the cave of the back seat trying to get my feet
to behave and not pummel Daddy's kidneys through vinyl the movie
of out-the-window tops of things and wondering do they really think
that guy is gonna eat crow and there goes Chicken Valley Road where
Jackie lives who is rich because instead of wet walls and power
tools her basement has a trampoline drop down turn around
find your way to heaven to the dentist's office is where we're going
like it or not just like everywhere my nose goes there are smells like
dogs make and Nana in her undershirt and stains that find always
the new dress and give me away for what I am a wide-faced snip-nosed
little Jesus loves me girl sweet like the sugar that rots my teeth but guilty

Be Properly Scared

"Be Properly Scared, and go on doing what you have to do." – Flannery
O'Connor (by way of Michelle Wyrebeck)

All week I practice letting her go, practice believing
the world will give her back. I run my hands over all
the allowable places. We tense watching Olympic girls
unable to stick their landings, eighty thousand flags
celebrating will. During commercial breaks, I answer
questions about pipe-bombs. Last night she was too
spooked to stay in the tent with only other kids. Last
night someone age 80 lay pulse-less on his floor and my
vice was sweetness, sleeping to the music of four stuffed
grape-leaf kittens mewling in their box. I wake up vacant,
but Della is a-swarm. *You sneak cigarettes*, she spits out,
fury turning to sobs: *I don't want you to have to go away.*

Interrogative

What was it you thought would fly
in the window? Was panic a confession,
wakefulness a miner's light under the blanket?
Do I need more ways to say love won't ever—
nope nope nope—be fractured by infractions?
How is your math coming along and what is
an algorithm? Will you forgive me if I die
from my own stupidity? Should I wait to tell you
maybe I do those things to make sure I die first?
Do you know I snitch candy from your stash?
Where in heaven did you get the phrase *sacre bleu*?
Did you have any idea, when you told me,
how huge and startling a gift it is that you trace
the lines of my face in the dark before sleep?

Another Something

In the trash bag I was swinging toward the car toward
the dump in a world of kitchen slime: a spear of broken jar
nobody could have known would sink deep into my leg
real easy, mingling its juices with mine, activating the body's
big words and little soldiers. All at once I'm wearing blood
and surprise, late to Della's piano lesson again: confluence
of hurry and music. I hear my mother's voice—slow
down, *Ode to Joy* is not a race, there's always something
waiting to happen. Seed waiting for water or an egg
to swim to; wood for flame; a child needing new lungs
waits for another child to die. The doc with an ironic smile
sews my leg and says sure the reason I tan fast is the years
in Brazil—it's called sun damage. It's called a rush to dubious
beauty, called another something lurking in the body's dark.

How to Look at Mother

Can you tell me how not to feel the way I do
when she says what kind of car is this
and it doesn't matter because then she'll say
it's a good car, no matter what? Can you
tell me why she can still sing the Doxology
perfectly but asks who is that man at the sink
and when I say that's Paul, that's my husband
Paul, can you tell me why her smile seems
all wrong, can you tell me why even now when
she has every reason for it she is still without
rage, or how mine (historically ready to hand)
has changed to disdain? Can you tell me how
to look at the woman in front of me and not
simply not see, but see more than what is left?

Almost

I almost sat on that raindrop, stopped
up her mouth for good—for shame!
Almost-but-not-quite got it—how to be
a daughter. Almost altogether bossy, almost
stayed giddy, almost placed a stranger's hand
on the breast that's almost yours, the nipple
that's almost hers. Almost fished for that
compliment but it flew up at me before I could
—exquisite timing! Then I almost morphed
into a luxurious mask again, just like I almost
convince myself each morning tonight
will be different: mood, volume, outcome.
I can see the almost future, but need something
more than eyes to banish that word. I mean
I almost lost you—almost didn't say nah
and put down the phone (and now I'm almost
telling, so you can almost give it to me)—darling!
If it ever really comes to that, I swear I'll
swear off all desserts, just or unjust, or mostly.

Cupped Palms

Some days the words I weigh in cupped palms turn
to ash, and what I really need is someone to tell me
the truth about trees. He was the one. Who'd bring me

back, hand-over-hand, from the parking lot, the wallpaper,
the well-meaning cul de sac. From the punishments I assign
myself out of habit, hearing their voices, *You've done it again*,

and for my crime: more this, less that, sign at the x. Still foggy,
I'd find him setting something silly and plastic in his fishbowl
and that was enough. Or I'd return from one of my expensive

trips to *How could you?* and there he was in the yard making
blisters on his hands. Awe and gratitude surprised him.
He was linen. My eyebrows would ask a question.

"We lash things together," he'd say. "Sometimes they float."

What You Know (Note To Self)

Everything liquid congealing, no lovely flame,
absence of red, this is the cold rage you imagine,
shoulders turned to granite, if you had 1982 to do
over, Elaine's mouth foreign across the table
saying "business decision," saying "nothing to do"
[beat] "with friendship," her lips borrowing stone
from your shoulders and you the earth the boulder
was shouldered out of, gaping open, thinking this
must be how divorce feels, who is this woman, upright,
glassy, insistent bowl thinking to be filled, remaining
empty, and she well knew you would not meet ice
with sizzling ice, calculation with calculation. What
you know, she'd never dream: you miss her smell.

Ghazal

Newly in my body, blind to the lie at the core,
I toy with forbidden self, tantalized to the core.

She leaves behind "creative movement" for pink
and a bun: how will she find her "I" in *the corps?*

Fire can't be small for more than five minutes. No
apology blooms from his mouth, I ignite at the core.

Are waves deaf? asks Michaux. Sometimes we covet
the most other of musics—craving a rise at the core.

Teen-angry, innocent of "it," I yelled *Eat it raw!*
In my underthings they found a good-sized apple core.

Kelly blades growing from cinders: (dubious?)
proof life there's life in what dies at the core.

For days she's years older, then sudden sobbing
and I'm lost to *my* effort not to capsize at the core.

Gutter is a word hurled: who lives there is tattered.
But aren't we owners uncivilized at the core?

Notes we fumble for, cracked melodies teased
up—hints for who listens: noise from the core.

I bloom to the thrill of a stranger, then flood

with blueish relief: he's not my size at the core.

Searching for seals, shells, shooting stars, we switch
from zoom to wide-angle, find we have eyes at the core.

In the wake of his leaving the island, foreboding—
but at dawn I still smell of last night at the core.

Dream: I eat the shelled egg a white hen offers held
in her claw-foot. Ellen, we are all disguised to the core.

Petals in the Dirt

Your words circle, mine batter. You're a ramp, I have
      no wheels. The kid who gets the brunt
of our love asks us not to bicker. Think
      of all the people who have lost their right
hands! The friend who says: Hug me twice,
      it could be a while till the next body
I can touch. Then there's the man who claims he wants
      steady, needs steady, but each woman's a lake
he's big enough to swallow. How will hunger like that
      ever learn to use a napkin? When you bring me
tenderness, it looks like one more thing
      I don't have time for. Maybe when it comes
to love, the happily long-married are the biggest
      fools. I'm fervent but off-and-on about my roses
—how many of us are delirious when the twenty-sixth
      blossom does its gorgeous thing? I wonder
if when I get home those petals will still be
      luminous and melting in the dirt. I'm thinking
maybe I need them. I'm saying what would I do
      without your mouth?

TWO

After the Lightning Bugs

What is there, once the lightning bugs go
inside their tiny invisible houses, and leave us

in the big dark? Twenty-odd years under
one blanket, for you to wake up hungry?

I used to float mornings in your nearby
absence, paper turning downstairs, chirpy

kid noise. Today's dream-drowse: I wake,
hand flung on the half-written, smudge-lovely

page of a child. I am not a vessel, hold nothing,
can't float, refuse to sink. I'm gutted, chilled,

shorn of seed. I turn toward the catbird's nonsense.
Across town, two people rise in unison, one of them you.

Two Months After News of Trouble in Paradise

I bring you my best words but they're always foreign

The newspaper brings news of infidelity among birds

Della brings me her hair to braid

You bring the weather report

Twenty times a day my right hand brings my death, red tip fuming

A dream brings your lover's consoling arms, I wanted to break them

Another brings the familiar man-in-hat-with-no-face

Our house is becoming my house

The need for a scrub brush arrives with a vengeance

Where's the leavening, the gate?

I don't care what dog comes along, I'll send his drool on its way

Someone came and cut a hole in the family photos

I don't care what tasteful thing N. brings, I don't want it

There's a circle of yellow the lamp brings the table for which I'm
ridiculously grateful

Mother can't remember what she meant to bring

My oldest friend calls with news of who I've always been

Baby animals are cute for a reason—haven't you looked at her lately?

Someone leaves a ripe tomato on the stoop

G. says "We are a strange species" and yes

Memory, oh revision, what can you bring me that isn't a demon puzzle?

If only morning didn't have to come, and November

I cannot bear to look in the closets

I come to this with only nine good fingers

The grass has stopped growing

Oh heating man, bring me a furnace!

Tomorrow promises a root canal

What other sorts of reaming out are on the docket

The crickets bring continuity for maybe another two weeks

What child is this?

I haven't sung in two months

Late light brings back my body for a moment

The house is sinking but wants to catch me

Sleep, even troubled, brings a certain kind of dove

It says: tomorrow bring home armfuls of—why not?—oleander—

Consider

How easily you let go the atticful of books,
loss preferable to visiting past lives, just

as you want to eat years of words—chew
and spit out. Ever mild, you sleep now

with a fierceness under your pillow.
But with what tenderness you regard

the fish on your plate, sweet with hoisin
and nothing you were ever married to.

Far From It

Far from the corn & hog state I still feel married to
where the in-laws are cooking for my replacement
Far from knowing the ropes, exactly needing one
Far from near to you, near to far

Far from a shepherd, you've scattered the sheep,
left me dung to burn, second-hand body heat
Far from two daughters, far from the cello in the next
room, any cello, are you nearer yourself?

From now on I'll always be where you're not
Here with my rough table, sand washing down the drive—
Drive—drive inside, please, beyond new shiny penny
and old friend gin, to who you might, near enough, still be

Go Deep

Dig five—no, ten years down to fresh earth
you will remember. Spade your slim
size, old barbells readied you, ground
welcomes. Deep, a decade ago you loved
your hurt hands, friends of rake and fork.
Leave aftermath, leave leaving, plant
yourself eye-level, sit with beetles and grubs
in the busy under-earth, the food of food
everything becomes. Forget the doings
up in the boozy light. Take, eat, get
sweaty, discover her comfortable father.

Prophecy

Your father was hungry for a last blast of light
so we hoisted his wheelchair into Aegean air

More rock and whitewash than tree or path
was the island of tending him in shifts

The road from where you sat to speaking of it
lay dark, even in that brilliance, a half-year away

You nursed silence, I blindness,
crossing to Delos without you

A prophecy, sun-touched and severed

House, the Verb

The body houses what the heart won't let loose
Loosening gives way to love
Oh birds happy in their feathers
Something sometimes happens
The heart's lurch, stop-and-go traffic
A crash course in tighten
That the house of us was an assumption!
Later houses what we never imagine
The way you flew from me
Wounded of wing, dusting chicken
What the I housed in belief
Unhoused, bereft of body

Match in My Fist

What about simply setting down the can
of gasoline, burying the rag? Please
not one more day with your spite
in my ears, the redundancy of tears
in the shower. No more road-smoothing
while you heave propellers, toiletries,
sandbags, spare change at my head.
You need your fire, your fire needs air,
I am blue with holding my breath.

Moving On

Thank you very much.
Dear. Thanks for all the
(hours) (months) (years)
you did not do
what you just did.
You may've been working
up to it, fairly bursting,
but, right-o, you stayed
buttoned. Sucked shut.
Thank you very much.
Or do I? Would you?
Is a sooner axe better
than the lie of continuity?
Is the much, the time you
did not do, due thanks?
I may have in snit said
spare me. I may have
snitted. You may have
thanked me very much.
Snit may betimes invite
snipe, wanderlust. We
have no x-ray of the (hours)
(months) (years) (praise
them) during which you
did not do. Though doing did
follow. Consider yourself
thanked. Consider me:
tuning up, ugly sudden

cicada. And you! No
longer sucked, plastered,
shut. (Newly sucked
and plastered.) I remain.
Moving on (hours) (months)
(years) before you can,
do. Think me very much.

No Moss

Why is the shed so full?
When did the fig tree grow too big for any of these rooms
like the heart in my chest when I'm driving?
No one asleep on the sofa you suddenly decided to hate—
your love has turned into what? A pebble!
In memory it is still a huge, sure stone.
How did it roll away
and which one of us was released from the cave?
For months now our mouths have had nothing
to do with each other,
but beans get cooked, wires inspected,
Palestine and poetry go on without you.
I've learned to shovel paths and fill buckets
with sand but not how to father.
There are people who mourn you, people who
cross you out. You drive around with spare tires
in your back seat. I sit in your chair,
small vengeance.

Ghost Disc

Where you live there's perhaps a thimble of me,
something tiny you meant to leave behind, nothing
I could see through the window

Where I live pins and needles are troublesome
but useful and we haven't put away
the happy pictures yet

How can it be that I want you unhappy?
Where I live the cellar dirt is packed, the air
impure with surprising music

You're cooking to Reggae with no thought
of our honeymoon, the Jamaican couple
admonishing us white folk to dance slower

I'm waiting to notice your first new shirt
I miss your hair, sometimes
it's as if no one else in the world has hands

Where I live nearly everything I touch has you in it
Where I live is a girl
I'll have to learn to lose, too

When I heard you'd taken to dog-walking
I heard ragged, shrewish barking in a neighborhood
called Sack of Limes and saw

a perfect sea bass skeleton flung
one Thanksgiving after another into the Brazilian sea
I have not replaced you as you have me

but that is my power
I thought I'd be afraid of the dark
but it turns out to be liquid, silver, trust

Sometimes my name must fall from your lips
I think I will change it
I am changing it

Will she keep you? What bears keeping?
The moment in Jerusalem you refused to buy me a ring
or the Armenians welcoming us to their blessed food?

Last night in my absence you slept here
breathing in tandem with our girl
How will I let that happen

where you live?
There were moments—years!—I felt my feet begin
to wander and followed them a little ways

I believed simply in the long road
I was not present for the death-toll of us
Do you live anywhere bravely singular?

Where I live sometimes there's a female cardinal
out the window, then a slim curve of moon
with that ghost disc behind it

THREE

Yes from No

When I decided not to drive my car clear through
    her new house and instead to look in, I saw
two place mats and oh the dinners he will make,
    saw the cookbooks wrenched out of my kitchen,
the sesame oil set back on the shelf empty, unthinking,
    the reason I scold him, the reason he's leaving,
the reason next time I drive by she's on the porch
    as if waiting for a man with suitcases to drive up,
my man, the gone one whose body still sleeps
    downstairs, and I also saw a dog I didn't like,
first mean, then goofy with its bone and drool
    at the back door grinning up like a goddamn
trained seal, but god help me I was for a minute
    demented—no, a screenwriter, pondering the ways
to kill a dog, send a little message, yes—in the movie
    version when I drive through her house, her dog's
exactly in my path, and I bust him through to the other
    side—how easily everything turns to slapstick or gore,
but in real life what punishment is there for this sin or that,
    my many omissions while they committed and
committed. I'm beginning to think the only punishment
    that counts is the kind handed down from the forehead,
handed up via reflux, finding its way somehow to set forever
    between the ribs like a kind of stitch, one in a line

of crooked stitches poorly sewn by our own child-hands
        because we used to know yes from no, sin from sin,
maybe it was the child in me that decided not to drive
        straight through them, the grown-up that said
go home and eat a pot of rice and get silly with my girl.

Sins of Grammar & Usage

We bookended you, and exhaled what we knew
would be fire, outlining your split-infinitive world:
a topic sentence so hot, running was your declarative.
Every everyday thing looked at you, useless, your tree
too full of caterpillars, the cellar door. You gave us
hours and days waiting on the shelf, as if punishing
with dark two toys who refuse to get along. You
gave us silence, then breakage, then subject-verb
with a lot of fuck in it.

He told you about the not-Mamma woman he loves,
I told you to sleep, sleep, you carefully folded your anger
and left it on his suitcase. You've made despise an active
verb. Who can tell you which love is what? Who can tell me
what grout is, where to take the garbage? This is the plate
he set before me three months ago, now it's your turn
not to eat. We "fucking idiots" say: this is not about,
because of, or on account of *you*, and you say the hell
with therapists and prepositions.

Now that we are two, I think you like all the scrubbing
I'm doing. You make allowances. When I can, I cook you
rice for breakfast, build a fire. My arms are often full of wood,
your fuse is lit, I miss his shoulders, I say Daddy's left me,
not you, I forget how to stir-fry. There's something here
about direct vs. indirect objects, the objects of our affection,
the not-me you are. We three are still a unit of grammar, yes,
radically modified, expletive deleted. This at year ten
is your sentence.

Parentheses

(Dear daughter, the first day I woke up knowing
he would walk away, they shot up the capitol,
I started to bleed, and all the butter in the house
went bad.)

(Dear One, the first day of my knowing this day
was coming was the first day I heard birds
before light. I thought: I just got stronger.
Also weaker.)

(The leaves are asking us to notice their last rites, almost
all smell and dust now, run-ons. You just got weaker.
Also stronger.)

(The way the branches dance their winter-coming syntax,
that's my kind of metrics. A bare, true love, the memory
of leaves, leaving, ellipses—like pooled ink where the hand
dozed.)

(Dear Della, everything lodged between parentheses eventually
comes out of its cave.)

House Made Larger

Today I'm wide enough to walk on, and not
minding—for the feet are young. Today I'm
full-spectrum, like a house made larger by fire.
I've never been so altogether cabinet, foxhole,
bathtub full of blankets; some synapse rings
a bell and the bell says gather, gather everything
in sight, line yourself every inch with extra
padding—pine needles, cloud wisp, piano noise.
Today is the first day everything about her
is my job. And, while I may be a raisin later
for a sad while, a stray thought of helium,
right now singularity has me double-barreled,
preheated, stockpiled and roomy—as big
and ready as her fierce love needs.

Daughter: an Apology

I'm sorry not to be every moment tongue
in groove, boot and lace, all you ever need.
I'm sorry you're the yellow wedge here,
the red over there, your pie illustrating
fractions never where you expect. Sorry
we have one percent instead of two, sorry
about every rash, each shoving midfielder,
all the daily dire. I hope to learn to hope
you can one day bring your heart along
to your other house. Yesterday I did
a little. Today, sorry, not at all.

Ever Since

Ever since the alarm went off, inconvenient feelings stirring,
outsized, unruly, trying to elbow their way in or out, restless
over the map of the day, trying the hang-dog, downcast eyes
routine, storming through your body, just like Della said
last week, sister in malady, pointing to her chest: *there's*
too much in here, and for as long as you keep your hands, legs,
mouth, and feet busy, ticker-tape brain ticking, they remain
a lozenge, a sourness pushing out an odor only you can smell,
refusing to dissolve—but just try to slip into the tub or behind
the wheel and you'll need more than the radio to beat back
the take-over, imminent domain, white line through wet lashes,
overblown heart blown open, floodgates and warning lights
and day-glo bumper stickers: emotion the size of a moose
planted in our path—ridiculous, undeniable, locally fatal.

Inside & Out

It's too bad love finds a way to seep out, whooshing
from the gaps between buttons, fighting like big water
down a small drain, slithering out from the secret crease
where the body promised the heart it would be safe.
What does the body know, with its insistent pump and
seethe, and all manner of life-or-death distractions?
Oooops, came up short today the closest to an apology
we get, or: *Life's a big sieve, get used to it.* Tell that
to the child who wears her love inside and out of her body.
You're bending me down like a too-tall piece of grass, I said
sharply, and thought I'd be sorry. But she said, *You make such
good similes!* Our tale is a small fish in light of the sea, but
when she cries, I say: *my wail is a pun and so is its blubber,*
words from a well, water of laughter. She doesn't break.

Also the World

There is my loneliness and there is
my daughter's—different breeds
that speak the same language of *I am*

ready. Boys will arrive with their hands.
My young beauty will trust them and I her,
and she will fly back, gusty, changed.

There is the way my feet know the stone
a dirt road becomes, detect first sponginess
once veins of ice seep, earth gives up

its grief. In spite of this and every gash
out of the blue, I whisk myself heel-through-toe
stirring the air. The ginger-cat who always

dashed uphill past barking, happy to flop
in roadsand at our feet will be gone,
is gone. What took her is also the world.

Did You Know

Della says that creatures deep in caverns have
neither eyes nor color. There was a princess

once who smothered under sixty pounds of silk,
and pollen is real heavy to the poor, straining bees.

False teeth are often radioactive, I offer. Ants stretch
when they wake up, and a rat can go without water

longer than a camel. Dirty snow melts faster than clean,
she counters. And the yo-yo was invented as a weapon!

Baby, some facts are worthy of both love and hate:
that there are in prison dreams. And what love is:

a wound that is no matter what in some way a gift.

As It Was

Dark as it was then, a wrenched
time, striding stranger to loss that I was
no longer, sitting in the bathroom simply
because it was small, shards of the gone
working their mocking way from inside
my body out,
though there was no blood
between us, though I wished for it,
blessed evidence, irrigation, something
to swim away in, dark as it was
I could see the dark was water
that would wash through me until it was through
and, even in the starless time
finding myself under the night umbrella
with mittens and a phone trying to keep
the worst of my shrieks from her small sleep,
dark as it was in the gathering change,
he not simply gone but mocking, me
no more or less deserving,
in her sleep
I could see myself,
striding, still blessed.

FOUR

You Get Up

You get up and wash your face
even if you will collapse by four
even if you can't imagine the face of God
even if life lately is eggshells and smoke.
The sky may be close with weather or launched a long way
into happy transparence. You get up
despite and because of the trip to the dump, the flat tire,
watch the man pull the nail, then hand it to you, memory
rightfully yours, some people like to keep them, he says.
Just as morning comes unbidden—too clean, too dirty,
eventually irresistible—you will come to your idea of heaven
and its host, singular or plural or singing.
Or—your last bodily morning (which you'll not recognize
in its everyday pain and beauty)—
you will not.
Today you wake certain you will survive
the man who left you.
You'll have to learn to lose him again, lose
your picture of the world with him in it
Maybe you'll have learned a love
like God's, flesh secondarily
and momentously.
In the mirror in the morning you follow paths
etched in your forehead or circling your neck
If God knew where they led would you want Him
to tell?

The Way Dawn

The way dawn leaks into the house: dark to glow
to daily. It doesn't matter who's upstairs sleeping
or not. Not like the tree that falls in the forest,
unless you believe in sound *sans* witness. Just as
no one's landlocked state refutes the sea. The sea
doesn't end; it sets us down on the ground,
and hurry doesn't end with stopping. These
were born simultaneously: my grief, my fury,
my freedom. What am I but the birth of not-you?
There's always something dawdling into dawning.
A door closes, a face feels the brief wind it makes
as a slap. Sting fades, then flares to knowing.
That man's wife died and we whispered how she
dragged him along. No. He found lovelight in the dark.

Forest to Stone

1.

On account of the mass of branches and their mess
of scrappy leaves, we figured we could live here
a while, worry about the unidentifiable later later.
Assume communion. Our work was what got tended.
But when I carved an intricate flute, you got a splinter.
You boiled the sky, but insisted it would be unlovely
to put the fabulous blue pigment to use. You cross, me
bossy. I said *You started it, stepping off the parallel.*
You said *You made me do it* and finally *Don't
forget who made you.* Or did I dream that, too?

2.

I'm cold, but I've never seen such marble. Eyes eat it,
skin wants its blinding slide. How could I gravitate
to such an empty place, not a shred of green? Why
draw near holy stone when I don't believe I believe?
Maybe I've been holding the picture upside down.
Tired of things each having their own color, I'll do
a while without a yielding world, live with sparse
when it's massive, dark, mottled, see music there.
Leave the forest in the forest, you in whatever light
you choose. Love something subtle and not my own.

Teeth to Grass to Branch

Something nameless is making waves—
The wounded bird is given back
from teeth to grass to branch.
In the canopy of the weed patch: tomatoes!
Mother can see, but she cannot say.
Not much solace, but she can smell:
grass, skunk, soap, wet.
Last night she held the phone right-side up
and said: Love you, too.
Her years of her evenness gave me
to the odd-numberedness of things
she is just now entering, unknowing.

Oh the busy city under the grass.
The dark it will make of our bone-white bones.

Mother is drifting fast, just as tufts
of milkweed begin growing their white hair,
and why shouldn't they? Now surrounds.
The birds are noisiest just before light takes
possession of the world. (It really does gather,
like dusk going the opposite direction.)
My skin shrugs off regiments.
The wind plays everything it can.
I have words, so I say: the irresistible
dented blue wheelbarrow waits.
We pass on the path.
The place I've never been is where I am.

Skein

The world throws me a skein, a loosely
twisted future. I must make a planet
in my hand. In my chest: lust and tangle.
I sleep alone and little. Memory says

it takes two, I say not yet, there is enough
two in my house, a twosome doing without
tango. A huge and sudden lack grabbed
my shoulders, turned me step-two-three

pragmatic. And then there's that tug
that says remember panoramic, then
zoom: the girl whose feet in Mozambique
are here today, gone tomorrow. The boy

in Sarajevo who can now perfect his header
in full sun. The horizon gives and takes
away. Does anyone who thinks hard
know what to do with the Lord?

In the end, it's not higher mathematics
but arithmetic that throws me. This new
duet trying to make sense of long division,
zero population growth, and a friend's cells

multiplying madly in her spine. Many

a holy fool sits straight in his chair
and claims otherwise, but art is no
idea, it's some kind of someone's yarn.

Rib(cage)

There's no way not to say this. His father did "x"
and didn't do "y." His mother was a creamy influence,

but then she went and died. All grown up, he was still
a smudge of a boy, no way to be a locomotive. He cut

the lace off the apron and put it on. He woke up married
and took it off. He traded the wife for a free-love painter

but they were doused in the 70s; it didn't last. When
the next wife arrived, she thought she'd found the true ark.

What wonderful tremors they made—but since she
opened the gate, how could she know he'd never scale

the walls? A barrage of good years they were lucky
to survive, then much clutching when a baby didn't come,

then came and uncame. When their wonder finally landed,
she was an eight-pound ovation he thought would never stop

—but then he hadn't counted on getting shorter. Hadn't he
hauled his share? Why should he say jump? Feel the barnacle?

Why shouldn't he tire of being a good listener when no one
noticed he'd gone mute? There's no way to say this.

His second wife did "a" and didn't do "b." His daughter

was a creamy influence but she would go and grow up.

Two too many mirrors. He had to take his funny ribcage—
the one he'd given her to remember him by—elsewhere—

Father Mine

What he thought went. Fast & far.
We feared him putting down his fork.
Mother smiled, mild beside a monolithic

given. She undertook. Move, stay,
was his to say. When did she begin
to nettle? Graduate to needle?

How he needed to lie down loose,
stayed taut, how she stayed, taught
softness. When did her mind

begin to leave? How he held himself
a body's measure apart, dancing.
When did the shepherd of unyield peel

fear to feeling? Now he must incite
laughter or she vanishes. How he spat,
Words are cheap, now lives for them:

"hero" from one son, exactly none from son
one. Judiciously he allows himself tears
and flying. Luxuriant, gives sweetness

to dishwater eyes knowing less and less
glimmer. Eighty-two today, neatly
exhausted, he is a rock relentlessly tender.

Circled by Water

The thing about the island is more hours, less
pretense. Here it's all bird-cry, stick snap, low growl
in something's mouth. At dinner I surprise myself
and say a blessing, something gone from me I can do
without. No need to wonder who was that girl I was,
content to hold the jib; all I can bear is the slow thrill
of now. Scavenging, what is it we look for to replace
what we've lost? Mother, newly a riddle, writes a letter
on the back of a garden, cuts it in half and sends only
the foreground, no Dear Ellen, no sky. The thing about
the island is there's a boat. I bring home fifty-seven
pounds of glass and beach brick, heather, bay, wild
mustard, good weight of stones, set it on the woodstove.
A heap of elsewhere, ballast that may teach a way to fly.

No Longer Mine

How many years will my mother go on passing
the anniversary of her subtraction, the day the first
piece of her slipped off into wet grass or got left
in the parking lot like a scarf lost at the end of winter

and not missed until the next? Why mourn the day
my daughter takes possession of her body—mother,
daughter, no longer mine as if they ever were? Who
flipped the switch from wishing to remember to trying

to forget? It's all recorded, each scintilla, memory dozing
until some rasp or whiff heralds its return and leads us
back without our knowing. Brain whorls are funny
that way, forever rearranging us—daughter opening

because she says so, mother a watercolor fading to plain
paper, not because of not remembering but because
her mouth no longer makes words; she lives beneath
her eyelids because she can no longer name the world.

Far Cry

Here I go measuring: new wrongs, old yardage, fat
content, computing the distance to heartache, stewing

over ferry schedule, minute hands, catch-of-the-day.
Why not do something useful, bring in the sheaves, tap out

syllables, bars of music, numbered loveliness? Something
shatters, requiring utility gloves and shard-count. How

can I be so shallow, cup and a half of lukewarm in a cold
basin? I have bags to hold bags. Some of my selves tread

lightly, testing the ice. They are not numberless. They catch me
unawares. They sit me down, these fractions, demand to know

what prompts this reckoning, rerecording, reiteration, such
poly-syllabic troubles. I abstain in three colors of ink. I abjure,

and reach for Webster's, the atlas, Napster, clutching everything
half-empty, almost-full. That's when it slips out, unreconstructed,

untranslatable, the skin's far cry for a clean hard wind,
boundless or not, to upend me, yes, sweep the table naked.

Between Us

I don't know how to wish you well.
Your hair is out of control, you are
downgraded and strange.You used to be

the man who whopped open his chest,
wandered on a happy shoestring, made
a nearly perfect girl. We were betimes

electric. Our battles were not over holy
ground; we only broke things we could
do without, walked off with barely

perceptible limps. Thinking ourselves a
perfect fit, we began to forget each other.
The way the roots of an over-watered lawn

get lazy. I thought my private fizzings
weightless. I thought we could both
get larger. You thought you should not

have to ask. What began as a secret scar
turned to decision, silence the size of my
thirst. Neither of us in twenty years truly

unlocked the other's body. Between us now
is paper, scissors, rock, one person's regret.
This is what I'll never tell: I took too many

days off from loving you. I'm ashamed
we failed at forever. Consider my iron
lung of a father, turned soft tissue, joshing

and washing the woman not quite still
my mother—a long tack in a small,
hand-made boat. I wish you, I wish me.

Good wood, even not together.

Late Red

The reddest thing is what we need to keep
hidden—to live—only red by surprise, exposed
to oxygen and our eyes. My leaving you
at the stove with damp hands I had no use for.
The way I've wanted to turn this into your hands'
fault. Into how you never learned to dip me.
Not how I averted my eyes, but how I was
(innocent) looking around and you (guilty)
found. Take back the hunk of you you left
(without knowing) when you left (without
my knowing). Twenty-five years and neither
of us quite got the steps down! Listen,
hydrate yourself back to life-size. Take
her love, these late tears, this red minute.

FIVE

Need to Know Basis

Instead of us, I'm wondering about the woman
in Afghanistan beaten by a mob for exposing an arm,
the face behind "need to know basis" and how
there's *scare* in *scarcely*. I'm wondering about

the widespread, the downbeat, about thread viruses
and how fear demands an object. The nerve!
I thought it was its own reward. Is there no way
to stand up to relativity? Out-select natural selection?

Let's just plain ban the word *deserve*. Cause of death:
one suspicious movement, complicated by black skin
and 19 bullets to the chest. We need to know
there are windows painted to keep women unseen,

and: when the medicine runs out, one doctor's thinking
that instead of watching his patients die he'll set them down
gently at the president's door. Here, in the meantime, the body
politic worries about (wants) fellatio. We have so many chickens,

pots to piss in, laps full of remotes, motes up the wazoo.
What do we offer even our local tragedies but ignorance & relish?
Like the foundry 20 miles from home—a taken-for-granted
brick wall blown away and into our talk for maybe two days,

then gone with the supermarket exec's 15 minutes of fame,
desk shaking in his lap, and the dozen ambulances with their seared
cargoes. Most of us don't know what a foundry is, never mind
the rule of nines. Or the smell skin can make. I'm thinking

we need borrowed moccasins, not insulation. Instead of
you-conjunction-me, I'm remembering the boy who shoved
a button up his nose. How he's still surrounded by ruin, baffled,
bringing himself up. Still biking his face around town, open to the world.

Clock Says

Clock says I haven't slept but two hours,
back says too much driver's seat, but what
does saying do? To be both rare and tender,
I need to walk it off, this blaring music,
these thoughts of not enough. I wish them
yours. I am altogether mined. An empty
bucket of wanderlust waltz. You found me

inconvenient, yesterday's blue sky, no
soap. On account of the reddening leaves
and your fibbing, my darning must be done
publicly, I am an element of style. The eye
of the beholder may be tired but it's not
only mine. Many there are who'd benefit
from at just the right moment a motherly

visitation, a white heap of dough to slap
around, the cool thwapping a preservative
of kindness, to be treasured as myrrh, taught
to second-graders, of which there are ever more
than we imagine in their corduroy singularity,
but those grooves, they're being laid down like
nobody's business, and we should make it ours.

Earth Is Where

Where strangers have tried to remove the mote
        from my eye, where I shouted them
down. Where pearls have been found
        among swine, blossoms in the muzzles
of big guns. Babies are tossed here
        into dumpsters and there are good laws
about certain feathers you cannot possess.
        We could do with less possession. To
divest ourselves of sharp-edged stocks, of vests
        and vestments. Not like trading papal chic
for black pajamas—let's find a we
        without uniforms: in our skin—dangerous
idea—in our sinews? Instead of his share
        of milk and honey, a Jew today—
unthinkable—took his leader's life. Every-
        where this killing, not just
each other but our own: in the belly
        of the great whale of a time we had
last night, in pissy hallways and nuclear
        split-levels alike. How many vigils
for our ventral earth, where whole or in bits
        we will be buried. Time to practice:
today silence, and tomorrow why not try
        to savor something that can't
be bought or fought over—a flame, a face,
        someone's first tear for another (tears,
the specialty of the species), for here we lie,
        so gathered.

Say Your House Shudders

Say your house shudders around your bed for a full minute
     and the radio says you're allowed to call it an earthquake
Say you follow your feet out into new grass, tufted and spurty
You see the drainpipe's harvest of pine leavings
You are thinking about a Jerusalem grocery
You notice the two new redbuds' moderate show of mauve
You imagine those two girls, one with a shopping list, the other a bomb
You see gravel blasting into bare limbs
Flash to how even mild winters mingle gravel with mulch
How windows film like aging eyes, weeds prepare to lift flagstones
Would there be any difference at all between the two mothers' keening?
How could Richter deface his wife and child, even beautifully, for an idea?
Is a dangerous act brave if you feel no fear?
Last year's Christmas tree lies passed out and balding beneath forsythia
The untuned orchestra of the grass tries Barber's Adaggio — no —
It's the shell of your ears echoing the webbed, unvisited shed,
     knotweed out back erupting from knuckles of trouble
Two hundred people behind church walls in Bethlehem for five weeks
     have not seen sky

Sunday Morning

The mullah wore beautiful shoes
Celery pickers don't get enough calories
Ice or snow arriving every Friday
In the western desert they paint pilgrimages on houses
The average Joe merits how many acres of junk mail
An eighteen-wheeler could potentially accordion as many cars
I wonder if they'll ever get that novelist
They're thinking of making the street one-way
The ice skaters are sharpening their blades
The public holds onto their hats, their stocks, their president
Downtown cannot be saved by skate-boarders
The latest storm hits elsewhere and on Thursday
Unnamed sources might just kneecap the reporters
Truck stop chapel does booming business
Another smiling athlete sees flashing metal
How much land was lost and where did it go
Finally, ripe tomatoes in mid-winter
Do you think we'll have a war

Anniversary

The day morning chill first
turns gentle, promising skin,

and soiled snow lies ignored,
old clothing. Rivers out-shout

worry in torrents. Sudden spray
on the radio—white hot nails—

today is the day, one year ago.
I was so close to the blast,

she says—waitress at the hotel
Seder—*no sound.* Life no longer

black & white—prayer & prey—
but our slow green, their sudden red.

Nothing about this is eternal, simply
returning. A long song, the year's

healing. They say the body
is the first drum. *I touched my jaw*

but it's not my jaw. My teeth are not
my teeth. Even my voice has changed.

On the Lawn

We turn from window screen to TV screen, watch
the doings in our name, no hope for an apology.
A man stands in the desert with a bucket. Everything
sweats—and are we the audience? Why is it called
the theater of war—burst after burst not equaling

sunlight? It seems to be about bunkers and big
helicopters, a relentless blast of misplaced pride.
Give up what you guessed about me. I have thoughts
but have not been tested. I am as small as the next
one. The President who doesn't know how

to be sorry. Page after page of better not say,
night after night leaning on a sandbag. No footage
of flag-draped coffins, much yardage of flag and tent,
fallow and fatigue. But how can we complain,
listening to casualty reports casually? How remain

seated, when we can't stand what we stand for: a war
preceded by an ad campaign. For every "freedom"
plug in "money." Take, swallow this slightly less
meaningful emotion. The reservist's wife says
he was to come home today—now what if

tomorrow? How can we let a mistake misspeak—
and for us: newsprint on hands, heads on pillows?
Some call it the sleep of the just, some wonder
if it's not bulldozing. The resister says it's tax
day—shall we? Whose job is this, (to weigh

or not to weigh)? Which one of us dares write
the script or play the gun? We don't say,
we pay and pay (only money, not our brother,
son, promise). It's groundbreaking all right—
pre-emptive emptiness. It's a condition to perform,

whose purpose is estate, not real. Landfills and
oilfields don't worry the rain. I have to say I'm
deeply sorry. Reservist, splintered sandbag, wife,
check in the mail. Sincerely yours. From here
in he-man's land. On the lawn a squadron of robins.

Our Species Alone

I swipe a rag across each leaf thick with gray,
thinking dirty house/bad person, thinking how

we tame everything, or try to, and wonder at our
success with dogs—how few, relatively speaking,

bite the hand that leashes them, how they're no
relation when they do, our species alone possessing

fire and euphemism, putting that dog "down"
or "to sleep," since of course our teeth don't flash

like that, but how many of us have watched a kid
poke a toad with a stick, watched a boy ride

his dog, a woman humiliate her child, and done
nothing, thinking glass houses, thinking stones.

The Road of May

It may be about opening
(what it is I need to know).
That when the lights came up
all I had in me was a sideways
glance is a clue. Oh the steel
doors I've been polishing. May
May be less strict than April
and me with it. It may be time
to be more deliberate! Why, faced
with an orchard, would anyone not
focus on a single tree? Crook
of barked arm, knobbed wrist,
spring fistful of yellow-green feathers!
But consider the dance we do, truly
looking only when the other's
not, talking to foreheads, noses,
furniture, our toes. Holding a gun
or a diagnosis, people look *where*
as they pull the trigger? No dive
into the eyes, smoothing a two-way
path. So help me, that's where
I may (half-century toddler)
shameless learn to walk.

Doing Is Believing

March into everything look for the hinge
Hit the beach of midlife as if at dawn
Entertain certain whims before weeping
Heed heartbeat entering untested hallways
Test becoming in unbecoming light
Seek beacon at dusk when stained beholden
Disdain stains produced by past impatience
Dream of meeting on the cusp mid-blunder
Don't hurry the girl bedding mid-promise
Don't bed your anger or launder your words
Wash your money in the day's true minute
Bow to child's-play worship silly and snow
Hail red clouds despite harm in the offing
Spite the past's dime-a-dozen things undone
Deny each tempting free pass to worry
Leap after tripping believing it song

First Date in Twenty-Five Years

Buttoning my sweater over the huge splotch
of white wine splashed to neutralize the coin

of red dribbled earlier in my nerves, I sit down
across from a man and find I've forgotten how

to use a fork. At home, I set the story we might make
beside the story I am making. To the first I give lots

of room and no punctuation; from the second I subtract
destruct, add *self*. Doze off feeling kissed. Morning

proper finds me weeping into bathwater: I must turn
into the one I've been threatening to become, faster.

January, Looking Around

The new wasn't born dancing, but who
is? Here at home I'm overcooked, dozey,

I've gone room temp. For god's sake,
ice crystals forming on freezer-burn

are more heroic. Parked, with a partial
view of the abyss, it's all I can do

to look at this rug. Neither danger nor
doorway (like my mother, dimly propped

another broken year). My feet are furious
and beauty is odd. The tin ceiling sheds

paint with impunity. The cherry trees
out back will, come spring, tempt cows

and shelter starlings. A pair of cleats
will clump mud and return my body.

Interviewing Herself, Midstream

Definitely. Age eight would've found me bruised
and beaming, by fifteen I was out of body and into

how to say it, la-di-dah, yes, singing, haranguing—even
a beseech now and again, huddled under dormers,

wriggling into wordskin while they painted the parsonage.
It adds up. But screw math, how could I be fifty ever,

much less in the year 2,000? You bet I counted, counted
on the impossible—Czech boyfriend, flowers in his hands,

one suit of clothes, Nixon in his closet. Never dreamed
the stage and my voice would fail me, that I'd take up my

pen: "Sweet immigrant, I loved you, but I need someone
more leery." Funny how later someone else got leery and I

got left. One ouch or another, what doesn't kill you, etc.
as they say. I say the house feels bigger-boned and it's my

turn to try a risk of air and feel small. As for my work—
I love the pieces, but it takes a tired lot of sewing. Yet.

Not a Sweater

An unmarriage is not a sweater half
unraveled or sheared in two not half
of anything not a husk or shed thing
or artifact behind glass or in the rubbish
not at the bottom of the sea calling out
nor tied to a chair with duct tape sealing
its mouth an unmarriage is not what one
or the other or anyone thinks not storm cloud
or tremor or even the sky finally in placid
agreement with the earth though like weather
it is not the air we breathe nor the mechanism
of breathing but irrefutably present in the gray
pink yellow bubblewrap of lung tissue in
perpetuity in the air pocketed down deep
not sustaining not part of the fabric
not dead

Slow Rapids

I'm somewhere between invisible
    and a congregation. Tomorrow still
on the other side of the planet, I'm looking
    to dance instead of tapping one foot.
The birds have eaten the path again, so
    I'm baking bread. The world is never
more or less ready, it's simply spinning.
    In the closed-for-renovations Dept.
of Romance, I am not my age. The saucer
    eyes I imagine into are not likely. Look
at me! Possibly *glasnost*, potential alpine
    meadow. As in tired tundra, as in rich
beneath the stubble. This snow isn't serious,
    it's in a flurry. But watch it gently clutch
and recline, at home in the limbs' digits.
    My fingers are busy rehearsing something,
my fabric admits the river. Tomorrow
    I'll have been alive fifty years. I'm some-
where between a current and a plate shift.

Per Se

Just past the mean purple briars that catch
jackets and scratch cars in this narrow dirt lane,
just as I near the steep leaf-glutted bank the neighbor
dog rolled herself down to die beside the cold rush
of river last year, I think of how I never think of sex.

The road has shrunk hard from sponge to plank to slab,
locking tight—metal shoulder to shoulder—the drums
of old oil that keep Vight from selling his garage, tidy
red lozenge between disorderly pines. I can go no farther.
The sun is doing that Biblical thing—throwing down

rays that promise Jacob's Ladder but deliver only
torment—well, not *per se* but we get the drift.
Oh, visible beams of light! Oh, unkempt spitfire
crouched in switch grass, alias tall panic grass,
it's not in the bed of night I long for a partner.

Warp of Door, Proximity of Darkening

Each waking shapes new noise, old water,
in a falling time. Downdraft of blue
and apple, though true, mean the same
bad thing while we praise them.
Scurry is in the air, up the nose, weighting
the freight. Something is lengthening
and it is not the day. We are one person
inside the rose of night. Dawn finds us
unfurnished. I beg my daughter to walk
backward and I continue my headlong,
twin impossibles who squabble. Listening
is the sky-sleep where decision is born,
slips toward cliff and, talking, spills into light.
The good is we need this sharpening.